SEVEN ROYAL LAWS OF COURTSHIP

*Practical Advice for Both
the Knight in Training
and the Princess in Waiting*

BY JERRY L. ROSS

Ultimate Goal Publications
stayinthecastle.com
(812) 665-4375

All Scripture from the King James Bible
Copyright © 2004
by Jerry Ross
All rights Reserved

Revised Edition:2020

Introduction

I have taught the Bible principles found in this booklet to teenagers for the past 20 years. There is no greater joy than to attend the wedding of one of your teenagers who has done it right. Watching two dedicated young people joined together in matrimony, preparing to serve the Lord together — well, it just doesn't get any better than that!

The principles contained in this book are founded on the Word of God. Not surprisingly, they are also in complete contrast to what is practiced by the world. Christian young people who mimic the world's unbiblical dating habits must often live with the heartbreaking results of ignoring biblical principles — loss of innocence and purity before marriage, and a coin-flip chance that they will still be married five years after their wedding day.

There is a better way. It takes courage and commitment to see it through, but the reward is the closest thing to Heaven a person can experience on earth.

Teenager, for this to work, you must be willing to enact seven laws that you will agree to live by. If you do, these laws will guide you past the snares of Satan and the pitfalls of your own humanity. If you have the courage to conduct your courtship according to biblical principles, you will be criticized and misunderstood by both the lost world and the carnal Christian. But you will succeed in finding that special one.

The Seven Royal Laws of Courtship

1. By the grace of Almighty God, I will marry the person God has created for me.
2. By the grace of Almighty God, I will arrive at the marriage altar morally pure.
3. By the grace of Almighty God, I will arrive at the marriage altar prepared to fulfill my responsibilities as a marriage partner.
4. By the grace of Almighty God, our marriage will have the blessing of both sets of parents and our pastors.
5. By the grace of Almighty God, I will have glorified God and

maintained an unquestionable Christian testimony throughout my courtship.
6. By the grace of Almighty God, I will give to my partner someone who understands and practices real agape love.
7. By the grace of Almighty God, on my wedding day, I will be in a position to fulfill God's specific calling for my life.

God is not the only one who has plans for your life. Satan will work feverishly to derail your dreams by offering you shortcuts and compromises. This "roaring lion" will play on your emotions and seek to pervert the natural desires God has placed inside of you. Compare the seven royal laws of courtship previously listed to Satan's goals for your wedding day listed below.

Satan's Seven Goals For Your Wedding Day

1. On your wedding day, Satan wants you to marry someone whom God never intended for you to marry.
2. On your wedding day, Satan wants you to have already experimented with sex.
3. On your wedding day, Satan wants you to be ill-prepared to make your marriage a success.
4. On your wedding day, Satan wants you to break your parents' hearts and grieve your pastor.
5. On your wedding day, Satan wants you to have ruined your testimony and to have brought shame to the name of Christ because of your unwise dating habits.
6. On your wedding day, Satan wants you to have no idea how to define or practice agape love.
7. On your wedding day, Satan wants your choice of a marriage partner to cause you to sacrifice the chance to fulfill God's calling on your life.

Sadly, I believe Satan and the demons of hell dance and celebrate at many a Christian young person's wedding. If Satan can cause you to miss God's perfect will in whom you are to marry, then he knows he has won a great victory.

Are you ready to examine the seven royal laws of courtship? Are you ready to pass them into law in your own life?

- Jerry Ross, 2020

1
First Royal Law of Courtship

"By the grace of Almighty God, I will marry the person God has created for me."

Every young person has a secret desire to be happily married. You may never talk about it, but it is there. You may never admit it to your friends, but when you are alone you dream about it. There is a married couple in your church whom you secretly watch. They obviously have a very close, sweet relationship. During public prayer, you peek (young people are great "peekers") at them. You watch as the man slips his hand into his wife's as they pray together. You watch them talk and see the love communicated through their eyes. You see the gentleness that the husband uses when he is with her and the admiration for him that she displays with every look. You think to yourself, *Is there someone like that out there for me?*

God has created someone specifically for you! This is one of the greatest of all Biblical truths.

"And the Lord God caused a deep sleep to fall upon Adam, and he slept: and he took one of his ribs, and closed up the flesh instead thereof; And the rib, which the Lord God had taken from man, made he a woman, and brought her unto the man. And Adam said, This is now bone of my bones, and flesh of my flesh: she shall be called Woman, because she was taken out of Man. Therefore shall a man leave his father and his mother, and shall cleave unto his wife: and they shall be one flesh" (Genesis 2:21-24).

Eve was created as the perfect fit — the perfect complement to Adam. God made a woman specifically for him. You must believe that the Lord God has also created someone just for you.

A part of you is in that specific one created for you. Eve had a part of Adam inside of her. God took a piece of Adam, a rib, and placed it inside of Eve. I believe that God has done the same for most every young person whom He ever created. Someone out there has a part of you in him or her.

You will never feel complete until you meet this person. The great mystery of marriage is this: How can two people become one? Yet God states that when two people marry, *"they shall be one flesh."* The answer is simple. Neither of the two were complete before they met. Both of them were missing a part of themselves that they could only find in the other. The divine longing that every young person feels — that incompleteness — is there because of how God made us. It is a desire to be whole.

God will bring this person to you. God did not wake Adam and say, "OK, I hid her in the garden somewhere. Good luck finding her!" Nor did God take six ribs and create six women and then say to Adam, "Date each of these and choose the one you like the best!" In His time, God brought the one made for Adam to him.

Notice, God caused a deep sleep to fall upon Adam: *"and he slept."* When God brought Eve, He woke Adam. In a real sense, God intends for young people to stay asleep in this area of their lives until the time God brings them to the one He has created for them. The world system — controlled by Satan — works hard to awaken a young person early. Hollywood movies, romance novels, rock and roll songs, teen magazines and an array of other worldly influences put a lot of pressure on young people to have boyfriends or girlfriends. All of that leads teens to believe that something is wrong with them if they are not involved with someone. This leads to roller-coaster relationships, one right after another, leaving a young person emotionally exhausted and morally vulnerable. Relationships like these are not sanctioned by God and have resulted many times in the loss of the purity of Christian teens. Relax! Rest! Be patient! And trust the Lord. He will bring to you His perfect will in His time.

Adam had to stay in the garden in order to meet Eve. Don't miss this! If you choose to leave the perfect will of God for your life, you sacrifice meeting the one God has created for you. This meeting will occur along the path of God's perfect will. Keep yourself pure. Save yourself for that special one. How serious it is to backslide! How perilous it is to choose to do what you want to do with your life instead of seeking God and His perfect will.

Your teenage years should be about preparation, not pursuit. As we will see in the chapters ahead, one of the primary activities of your teenage years should be preparing for the one God will someday bring to you. Begin now to pray for that person even though you probably don't know as yet who that person is.

"But How Will I Recognize the One God Created for Me?"

This book is written to give you Bible principles that will help to guide you to this person. When the time comes, God will let you know. But remember this: he/she is not the one if you have to sacrifice any of your seven biblical goals in order to "make it work." Here are a few suggestions that will help you know and recognize God's perfect will — and be wise enough to recognize a counterfeit sent by Satan.

1. God's perfect will is discernable only to those who have dedicated their lives to the Lord.

"I beseech you therefore, brethren, by the mercies of God, that ye present your bodies a living sacrifice, holy, acceptable unto God, which is your reasonable service. And be not conformed to this world: but be ye transformed by the renewing of your mind, that ye may prove what is that good, and acceptable, and perfect, will of God" (Romans 12:1-2).

God makes clear His good, acceptable and perfect will to you only if you are willing to present your body as a living sacrifice to Him. By the way, this is not an unreasonable request on the part of God. He made you, and He bought you with His Son's own blood. To refuse to dedicate yourself to God prevents you from discovering God's perfect will for your life.

2. God's perfect will is discernable only to those who have transformed their minds from worldly thinking to Biblical thinking.

"...but be ye transformed by the renewing of your mind, that ye may prove what is that good, and acceptable, and perfect, will of God" (Romans 12:2).

If you are to discover God's perfect will, He has a second requirement: you must learn to think differently. The young person who learns to think Biblically — who learns to see things from God's perspective — becomes capable of recognizing the perfect will of God. Your mind will be renewed daily as you spend time in God's word and meditate on those truths you discover.

3. No unsaved person should ever be considered a potential marriage partner.

"Be ye not unequally yoked together with unbelievers" (II Corinthians 6:14).

Did you know that the main reason God sent the Old Testament flood to destroy the world was because of Christian young people making the foolish decision to marry unbelievers?

"And it came to pass, when men began to multiply on the face of the earth, and daughters were born unto them, That the sons of God saw the daughters of men that they were fair; and they took them wives of all which they chose. And the Lord said, My spirit shall not always strive with man, for that he also is flesh: yet his days shall be an hundred and twenty years. There were giants in the earth in those days; and also after that, when the sons of God came in unto the daughters of men, and they bare children to them, the same became mighty men which were of old, men of renown. And God saw that the wickedness of man was great in the earth, and that every imagination of the thoughts of his heart was only evil continually" (Genesis 6:1-5).

Here, briefly, are the events leading up to the Old Testament flood. Two civilizations emerged from Adam and Eve. The descendants of Cain created a civilization where God was excluded. The descendants of Seth, on the other hand, created a civilization where Jehovah God was honored and worshipped. For many generations, these two civilizations had little or no contact.

At some point, each grew and expanded to the point where there began to be increased contact between these two groups. The young men who were descendants of Seth began to notice the young ladies from Cain's lineage. They began to pursue them because of one stated reason: "they were fair," meaning they were appealing to the eyes and to the flesh. Years before, Cain's civilization had left behind decency and virtue. Like many young women of today's world, they had been raised with the dangerous notion that the way to attract men was through immodesty and seduction. They wore less, but they were also worth far less.

God's reaction to His children marrying the worldly, lost inhabitants of earth was anger. (It is still His reaction today!) He was so angry that He immediately shortened the average life span of mankind to 120 years. That may still seem like a lot of years, but remember, Adam lived to be 930 years old. If we use his age as a benchmark, God reduced man's life span by 87%!

Did the children of these unscriptural marriages grow up to serve the Lord? NO! Just the opposite is true, for the Bible describes the next generation in sad and frightening terms. *"And God saw that the wickedness of man was great in the earth, and that every imagination of the thoughts of his heart was only evil continually. And it repented the Lord that he had made man on the earth, and it grieved him at his heart. And the Lord said, I will destroy man whom I have created from the face of the earth...for it repenteth me that I have made them"* (Genesis 6:5-7).

When a Christian young person marries an unsaved young person, it grieves the heart of Jehovah God.

4. No one should be considered who claims to be saved but who refuses to dedicate himself/herself to the Lord and separate from worldliness. This is true because...

An undedicated and unseparated young person might not really be saved. *"Wherefore by their fruits ye shall know them. Not every one that saith unto me, Lord, Lord, shall enter into the kingdom of heaven; but he that doeth the will of my Father which is in heaven"* (Matthew 7:20-21).

You have no way of looking into the heart of another young person to know whether or not he/she is truly saved. So you must inspect his/her life to see what it produces. The outward appearance, actions and attitudes make up a young person's *fruit*. Anyone can talk the talk, but a person who is really saved will have the outward evidences of an inward conversion. If I do not see in a young person a desire to draw close to the Lord — and in doing so, draw away from worldliness — then I should not just assume that he/she is saved.

An undedicated and unseparated young person cannot know God's will for his/her life even if he/she is saved. As we already pointed out, those unwilling to dedicate themselves to the Lord and transform their worldly thinking are incapable of discovering God's perfect will for their lives. Do you really want to marry someone who cannot discern his/her divine purpose?

The unwillingness to dedicate his/her life to God exposes a character weakness. He/She may not be willing or able to dedicate himself/herself to you.

The unwillingness to separate himself/herself from the world exposes another character flaw. Will he/she separate himself/herself only unto you? If someone cannot be true to a perfect God, will that person be true to an imperfect companion?

If you are a dedicated Christian, your children will not have a unified example in the home. *"My son, hear the instruction of thy father, and forsake not the law of thy mother"* (Proverbs 1:8). Question: how can your child obey this verse if his parents are teaching — by words and example — two different things?

You risk becoming a victim of divorce. *"Can two walk together, except they be agreed?"* (Amos 3:3). There is one thing two people must agree upon if they are going to walk together. They must agree to walk the same direction. Many a Christian young person has settled on marrying someone who was not a dedicated Christian and has determined that he/she would be able to change his/her mate after marriage. Most end up either backsliding and living just like the mate or divorcing.

My young friend, God has created someone just for you! Will you exercise the patience and wisdom needed to allow God to bring you to that person along the timetable of His perfect will? Will you enact the First Royal Law of Courtship as the law of your life? *"By the grace of Almighty God, I will marry the person God has created for me!"*

2

Second Royal Law of Courtship

"By the grace of Almighty God, I will arrive at the marriage altar morally pure."

The Christian world abounds with horror stories when it comes to young people and immorality. Any pastor in America could tell multiple illustrations about Christian young people who blew it when it came to preserving their purity. Some Christian leaders have lowered the standard and have even suggested that premarital sex is just a given nowadays and not that big of a deal. The Word of God, however, clearly outlines God's standard and warns of the consequences of ignoring it.

"Thou shalt not commit adultery" (Exodus 20:14).

"Flee fornication. Every sin that a man doeth is without the body; but he that committeth fornication sinneth against his own body" (I Corinthians 6:18).

"For this is the will of God, even your sanctification, that ye should abstain from fornication" (I Thessalonians 4:3).

"Marriage is honourable in all, and the bed undefiled: but whoremongers and adulterers God will judge" (Hebrews 13:4).

Don't let Satan deceive you! Not everyone is "doing it." An army of Christian young people across America are preserving their purity as a gift they will someday give to the one God has created for them.

How can a young person live by the *Second Royal Law of Courtship* in the midst of an "if it feels good, do it" world?

1. Make a vow of chastity to the Lord. This is a solemn promise, a vow to the Lord, a commitment to keep yourself pure until your wedding day. Read the following verse carefully. This is the right thing to do, but be warned: God will hold you to your vow.

"When thou shalt vow a vow unto the Lord thy God, thou shalt not slack to pay it: for the Lord thy God will surely require it

of thee; and it would be sin in thee" (Deuteronomy 23:21).

2. Realize the battleground for purity is fought in the mind. Work at developing a pure mind. First, let's be reminded that we are commanded to have a pure mind and heart. God would not command us to do something without giving us the power and ability to do it.

"Flee also youthful lusts: but follow righteousness, faith, charity, peace, with them that call on the Lord out of a pure heart" (II Timothy 2:22).

"Beloved, now are we the sons of God, and it doth not yet appear what we shall be: but we know that, when he shall appear, we shall be like him; for we shall see him as he is. And every man that hath this hope in him purifieth himself, even as he is pure" (I John 3:2-3).

Guard your eye gates! The mind collects information sent to it from many sources — sight, sound, smell, touch, taste — but most of the information is collected through a person's eye gates! You must be careful what you look at each day.

"I will set no wicked thing before mine eyes" (Ps 101:3).

"I made a covenant with mine eyes; why then should I think upon a maid?" (Job 31:1).

"How do I deal with evil thoughts?" Many times I have had young people come in need of advice on how to overcome the wrong kind of thoughts. The answer is simple: our wonderful Creator has equipped us with minds that cannot think on more than one thing at a time. Paul instructed the Romans, *"Be not overcome of evil, but overcome evil with good"* (Romans 12:21). You choose to meditate on "whatsoever things are pure" and, in doing so, you cast down evil imaginations and bring every thought to the obedience of Christ. Scripture memorization and meditation will always overpower evil thoughts.

"Finally, brethren, whatsoever things are true, whatsoever things are honest, whatsoever things are just, whatsoever things are pure, whatsoever things are lovely, whatsoever things are of good report; if there be any virtue, and if there be any praise, think on these things" (Philippians 4:8).

"Casting down imaginations, and every high thing that exalteth itself against the knowledge of God, and bringing into

captivity every thought to the obedience of Christ" (II Corinthians 10:5).

"Thy word have I hid in mine heart, that I might not sin against thee" (Psalm 119:11).

"But his delight is in the law of the Lord; and in his law doth he meditate day and night" (Psalm 1:2).

Never make excuses for lusting after the opposite gender. Doing so is a sin. It is condemned in the Word of God again and again. If you are having problems in this area, God can give you victory! Again, you must protect your eye gates. Satan is using television, Hollywood movies, DVDs and videos, the Internet and teen magazines to bombard your generation with explicit, sinful images. You need to eliminate these influences from your life.

"Then when lust hath conceived, it bringeth forth sin: and sin, when it is finished, bringeth forth death" (James 1:15).

"For the commandment is a lamp; and the law is light; and reproofs of instruction are the way of life: To keep thee from the evil woman, from the flattery of the tongue of a strange woman. Lust not after her beauty in thine heart; neither let her take thee with her eyelids" (Proverbs 6:23-25).

"But I say unto you, That whosoever looketh on a woman to lust after her hath committed adultery with her already in his heart" (Matthew 5:28).

"Love not the world, neither the things that are in the world.... For all that is in the world, the lust of the flesh, and the lust of the eyes, and the pride of life, is not of the Father, but is of the world" (I John 2:15-16).

3. Institute a personal "no-touch rule" and enforce it.

A personal no-touch rule means that you do not touch members of the opposite gender who are not immediate family, nor do you allow them to touch you. The Bible tells us that this will guard you against fornication.

"Having therefore these promises, dearly beloved, let us cleanse ourselves from all filthiness of the flesh and spirit, perfecting holiness in the fear of God. Receive us; we have wronged no man, we have corrupted no man, we have defrauded no man" (II Corinthians 7:1-2).

"Now concerning the things whereof ye wrote unto me: It is

good for a man not to touch a woman. Nevertheless, to avoid fornication, let every man have his own wife, and let every woman have her own husband" (I Corinthians 7:1-2).

A personal no-touch rule requires you to build relationships based on friendship and respect instead of lust and selfishness. If a young man or a young lady claims to love you, then they will be committed to protecting your purity and your reputation.

It is impossible to maintain a pure mind without maintaining a high standard of physical restraint. No young person can handle a member of the opposite gender without stirring his/her own personal passions. We are commanded in the Bible not to defraud one another. Defrauding another means to stir up desires within them that cannot be rightly satisfied.

"For this is the will of God, even your sanctification, that ye should abstain from fornication: That every one of you should know how to possess his vessel in sanctification and honour; Not in the lust of concupiscence, even as the Gentiles which know not God: That no man go beyond and defraud his brother in any matter: because that the Lord is the avenger of all such, as we also have forewarned you and testified. For God hath not called us unto uncleanness, but unto holiness" (I Thessalonians 4:3-7).

The time to develop a physical relationship is after marriage, not before. *"To every thing there is a season, and a time to every purpose under the heaven...a time to embrace, and a time to refrain from embracing"* (Ecclesiastes 3:1...5).

"Marriage is honourable in all, and the bed undefiled: but whoremongers and adulterers God will judge" (Hebrews 13:4).

One step of romantic physical contact will lead to the next: holding hands→hugging→kissing→petting→ruined testimony.

I recently read in *USA Today* that 85% of single 17-year-olds admitted to having already lost their purity. If Christian young people insist on following the dating standards of the world, then they will live with the results of those standards. On the other hand, 100% of young people who institute a personal no-touch rule and enforce it arrive at the marriage altar morally pure. 100%!

4. Never place yourself in a situation that increases the temptation or the opportunity to be immoral. Never be alone or isolated as a couple.

"But put ye on the Lord Jesus Christ, and make not provision for the flesh, to fulfil the lusts thereof" (Romans 13:14).

There has been much written in recent years concerning the difference between dating and courting. Let me summarize the difference. **Courting** is developing a relationship with an individual in the safety of a group. **Dating** involves a couple isolating themselves from others and thus leaving themselves open to temptation. The world's dating philosophy has robbed many young people of their purity. Don't date alone in a car. Never be alone in either of your parents' homes. Stay in the safety of good Christian company. Isolation increases temptation and provides opportunity: it makes "provision for the flesh, to fulfill the lust thereof."

5. Understand the importance of "pacing" a relationship. This is essential in helping you arrive at the altar pure and chaste.

In order to properly pace a relationship you need to answer these questions:

What is the age a serious relationship should start?

What is the earliest marriage should be considered?

How do I pace a relationship so that it will peak at the targeted time for marriage?

I am going to offer here some practical advice based on Bible principles, common sense and over twenty years' experience working with teenagers. Some parents allow their teenagers to ride the romance roller coaster. Many let them start in junior high school or even before, allowing them to become involved in one dead-end romantic relationship after another. These "practice relationships" leave young people emotionally scarred and vulnerable. Please consider the following suggestions.

Spend your high school years serving the Lord, making friendships and preparing yourself for your future.

Do not get into a serious boy-girl relationship during your high school years. When you graduate from high school, you should have all of your options open. There will be an enormous difference between how you look at life on the day you turn sixteen years of age and how you view it on the day you turn twenty-one. I believe that there is no five-year period in life in which a person's view of life changes more than during those five years. I personally believe that most young people would be wise to wait until the end of that five-year period before pursuing a serious relationship.

Most romantic relationships peak in intensity within a two-year period. What I mean by that is, after two years, you have exhausted every level that a proper relationship can rightly achieve and are ready to be married! If this is true, why start a serious relationship five years before you should be married?

If you do not properly pace your relationship, you will peak before you should and one of the following will happen:

You will get married before you should.

You will break up with that person out of frustration.

You will create unnecessary immoral temptations.

None of these three leads to personal happiness, so exercise patience during your teen years. Let little steps be big ones. Enjoy all phases of your life. Build many friendships during your teen years and leave it up to God to develop one of these friendships into something more in His time and according to His perfect will.

6. Have a game plan.

Age 13-18: "I'm not going to get caught up in riding the romance roller coaster. God has someone He is preparing for me, and during these years I will prepare for that special one."

Age 18 and beyond: "The time has come to prayerfully consider other dedicated Christian young people as a possible partner for life. I will rely heavily upon the counsel of my parents and the Holy Spirit's leading. I refuse to get in too big of a hurry. I will begin preparing to accomplish what God has directed me to do. When God leads me to this one, I will pray for great wisdom in pacing our relationship so that we both enjoy each step as God turns our friendship into divine love."

The Anatomy of a Seduction

The Bible devotes an entire chapter to an eyewitness account of the seduction of a pure young man. Whether you are a young man or a young lady, you can learn much by examining the mistakes that he made and that led to his downfall. Open your Bible to Proverbs, chapter 7, and then consider carefully the following principles designed to protect you from the scarlet sin.

1. Don't stay simple.

"*And beheld among the simple ones, I discerned among the youths, a young man void of understanding*" (Proverbs 7:7).

Make the attainment of wisdom the primary goal of your teenage years. (Read the chapter on attaining wisdom in the author's book *The Teenage Years of Jesus Christ*.) Wisdom is a shield, a protection against immorality. A person who remains simple is an easy target.

"*Get wisdom, get understanding: forget it not; neither decline from the words of my mouth. Forsake her not, and she shall preserve thee: love her, and she shall keep thee. Wisdom is the principal thing; therefore get wisdom: and with all thy getting get understanding. Exalt her, and she shall promote thee: she shall bring thee to honour, when thou dost embrace her*" (Proverbs 4:5-8).

"*My son, keep thy father's commandment, and forsake not the law of thy mother: Bind them continually upon thine heart, and tie them about thy neck. When thou goest, it shall lead thee; when thou sleepest, it shall keep thee; and when thou awakest, it shall talk with thee. For the commandment is a lamp; and the law is light; and reproofs of instruction are the way of life: To keep thee from the evil woman, from the flattery of the tongue of a strange woman*" (Proverbs 6:20-24).

"*When wisdom entereth into thine heart, and knowledge is pleasant unto thy soul; Discretion shall preserve thee, understanding shall keep thee: To deliver thee from the way of the evil man, from the man that speaketh froward things...To deliver thee from the strange woman, even from the stranger which flattereth with her words*" (Proverbs 2:10-16).

2. Avoid places of temptation.

"*I discerned among the youths, a young man void of understanding, Passing through the street near her corner; and he went the way to her house*" (Proverbs 7:7-8).

This was no accident. He "went the way to her house." It is foolish to purposely put yourself in a place of increased temptation. Remember the Lord's prayer: "*...lead us not into* *temptation....*" The young person who seeks out temptation, having convinced himself that he is strong enough to withstand it, shows no wisdom at all and will eventually become a casualty.

"A prudent man foreseeth the evil, and hideth himself; but the simple pass on, and are punished" (Proverbs 27:12).

3. Avoid hours of temptation.

"In the twilight, in the evening, in the black and dark night" (Proverbs 7:9).

A good rule of conduct is a simple one: when the street lights start to come on, it's time to go home. The Devil loves the night-time hours and does most of his work under the cover of darkness.

4. Avoid those who dress immodestly.

"And, behold, there met him a woman with the attire of an harlot" (Proverbs 7:10).

When Adam and Eve sinned, they sewed fig leaves together "and made themselves aprons." When God found them, he slew an animal (the blood sacrifice) and made them coats. Man's idea of clothing was aprons (literally, loincloths), and God's idea of modesty was to cover them from their shoulders to their knees. It is sad to say that ever since then, mankind has been fighting to get the apron back!

In Mark, chapter five, when the maniac of Gadara was delivered from the influence of demonic possession, he was found at Jesus' feet, "clothed, and in his right mind." Satanic influence always encourages nakedness, but true conversion leads to right thinking which, in turn, directs a person towards modesty.

How Christian young people (or adults) can read what the Bible says about immodesty and nakedness and then try to defend their right to "dress anyway they want" is ridiculous! Avoid those who dress immodestly. They do it for a reason, and they are sending a clear signal.

5. Avoid people of low moral character.

"And, behold, there met him a woman with the attire of an harlot, and subtil of heart. (She is loud and stubborn; her feet

abide not in her house: Now she is without, now in the streets, and lieth in wait at every corner.)" (Proverbs 7:10-12).

You can identify people of low moral character by their actions. Watch out for young people who are deceitful ("subtil of heart"). If they are always trying to sneak behind their parents' backs or pull the wool over the eyes of their pastor, watch out!

Two bad habits for any young person, boy or girl, are to be "loud and stubborn." All of us at times get a little rowdy, but notice here that being loud is connected with stubbornness. Mark and avoid that young person who always wants to argue with those in authority!

Loitering reveals a lack of purpose. People who waste time are wasting their lives. Compare this to young people who have direction and who use their time to better themselves and serve others. Be cautious of forming friendships with anyone who hates to be at home with his own family or who always wants to run the streets. Idle hands are still the Devil's workshop.

6. Avoid people who cannot keep their hands to themselves.

"So she caught him, and kissed him" (Proverbs 7:13).

"Oh, she is just overly friendly. She likes to touch you when she talks to you."

Right.

"Oh, he doesn't mean anything by it."

Don't be so simple. People who cannot talk to you without putting their hands on you are sending a clear message. Be wise and avoid them!

7. Avoid people who wear a cloak of spirituality.

"...and with an impudent face said unto him, I have peace-offerings with me; this day have I payed my vows" (Proverbs 7:13-14).

The most dangerous young people in the world are young people who at one time were in church and picked up just enough of the lingo to deceive a Christian teen into thinking they are also "religious" or "saved." Notice these startling verses found earlier in the Book of Proverbs:

> *"Discretion shall preserve thee, understanding shall keep thee: To deliver thee from the way of the evil man, from the man that speaketh froward things; who leave the paths of uprightness, to walk in the ways of darkness...To deliver thee from the strange woman, even from the stranger which flattereth with her words; Which forsaketh the guide of her youth, and forgetteth the covenant of her God"* (Proverbs 2:11-17).

Young ladies, notice that when God warns you of the evil man, he tells you that at one time he left the paths of uprightness. Young men, notice that the strange woman forsook the guide of her youth and turned her back on a covenant she had once made with God. Both of these dangerous individuals had some religious training. They both had a church background. Don't be fooled by those who can talk the talk. Watch what they do! Are they living for God now? Use some discretion. Exercise some godly understanding. Don't be simple!

8. Avoid those who talk suggestively or use flattery and fair speech to get what they want.

> *"Therefore came I forth to meet thee, diligently to seek thy face, and I have found thee. I have decked my bed with coverings of tapestry....With her much fair speech she caused him to yield, with the flattering of her lips she forced him"* (Proverbs 7:15-21).

She lied. She did not seek him specifically. She was waiting for any foolish young man who was silly enough to ignore Bible principles and put himself in a place of temptation.

She began to talk about things that no one should talk about except with her marriage partner. She began to suggest and seduce. Beware of young people who want to talk dirty or are always saying things that are borderline, things that carry a double meaning. It is never appropriate for a young person to talk to a member of the opposite gender about the subject of physical intimacy. It is inappropriate and, if one does, it is because there is an ungodly motive for doing so.

She began to use flattery. Proper compliments are usually directed at a person's character or spirituality. Flattery is a compliment with an ulterior motive. It usually is directed at a person's physical attributes and is intended to stir his or her pride and passions.

Avoid people who make you uncomfortable by talking

about things that are private and intimate. Avoid those who use compliments as a way to control you or manipulate you — and never trust someone who is a habitual liar!

9. Avoid people who are always trying to get you alone.

"For the goodman is not at home, he is gone on a long journey: He hath taken a bag of money with him, and will come home at the day appointed" (Proverbs 7:19-20).

"Come on over this afternoon. My dad will be at work and my mom is going shopping." Go ahead and refuse that invitation. A decent young man would not invite a young lady to his home when there would be no supervision. No decent young lady would suggest that you come over when she is home unchaperoned. For the sake of your reputation, never put yourself in that situation.

10. Read often the consequences of fornication and adultery.

"He goeth after her straightway, as an ox goeth to the slaughter, or as a fool to the correction of the stocks; Till a dart strike through his liver; as a bird hasteth to the snare, and knoweth not that it is for his life. Hearken unto me now therefore, O ye children, and attend to the words of my mouth. Let not thine heart decline to her ways, go not astray in her paths. For she hath cast down many wounded: yea, many strong men have been slain by her. Her house is the way to hell, going down to the chambers of death" (Proverbs 7:22-27).

The biggest lie Satan is feeding to the human race is that immorality no longer comes with a price tag. I understand that God is a forgiving God. He will honor His word and remove the sin of immorality from anyone's eternal record if that person repents. But there are built-in consequences — physical, emotional and spiritual — that you will live with the rest of your life. Read carefully the following verses, reminding yourself as you do that these are God's words and He is not a liar.

"To deliver thee from the strange woman....For her house inclineth unto death, and her paths unto the dead. **None that go unto her return again, neither take they hold of the paths of life***"* (Proverbs 2:16-19).

"My son, attend unto my wisdom, and bow thine ear to my understanding: That thou mayest regard discretion, and that thy

lips may keep knowledge. For the lips of a strange woman drop as an honeycomb, and her mouth is smoother than oil: **But her end is bitter as wormwood, sharp as a twoedged sword. Her feet go down to death; her steps take hold on hell***"* (Proverbs 5:1-5).

"And why wilt thou, my son, be ravished with a strange woman, and embrace the bosom of a stranger? For the ways of man are before the eyes of the Lord, and he pondereth all his goings. His own iniquities shall take the wicked himself, and **he shall be holden with the cords of his sins. He shall die without instruction; and in the greatness of his folly he shall go astray"** (Proverbs 5:20-23).

"For the commandment is a lamp; and the law is light; and reproofs of instruction are the way of life: To keep thee from the evil woman, from the flattery of the tongue of a strange woman. Lust not after her beauty in thine heart; neither let her take thee with her eyelids. For by means of a whorish woman a man is brought to a piece of bread: and the adulteress will hunt for the precious life. **Can a man take fire in his bosom, and his clothes not be burned? Can one go upon hot coals, and his feet not be burned?***.... But whoso committeth adultery with a woman lacketh understanding:* **he that doeth it destroyeth his own soul. A wound and dishonour shall he get; and his reproach shall not be wiped away"** (Proverbs 6:23-33).

3
Third Royal Law of Courtship

"By the grace of Almighty God, I will arrive at the marriage altar prepared to fulfill my responsibilities as a marriage partner."

Weekly wedding announcements appear in our local newspapers. Smiling pictures of young romantics, their eyes full of love and anticipation, stare at us from the page. If we wanted to, we could clip out every other one we read about and tear it in half. As cruel as that sounds, statistics tell us that over half the young couples who exchange wedding vows this year will have their marriage end in divorce. The percentages of those who then remarry and again end up divorced are even higher.

There is not a family out there who has not been touched by divorce. Perhaps "touched" is too kind of a word. "Pounded" might be more appropriate. No one ever wins — not the couple who goes through it, not their extended families and certainly not the children involved.

There are many reasons why marriages fail. One of the most often repeated phrases I have heard when counseling with victims of divorce: "The honest truth is neither of us were ready for marriage." Often young people were not ready because, instead of having spent their teenage years preparing themselves for the future, they invested their energy and emotions into one dead-end relationship after another.

Wise young people realize that their teenage years should be spent preparing themselves for the future. Teenagers who are patient and who decide to trust God will spend their time preparing themselves for the future so that when God does bring that special one into their lives, they will be ready.

The Prepared Young Man

I want to challenge you to prepare yourself now so that you will be a successful husband and father later. Managing a successful home may look like a breeze, but it isn't. Taking a wife and establishing your own family are huge responsibilities. It takes foresight, planning and preparation.

Before you say "I do," you should be able to honestly say three other things:

"I am prepared to lead."

Before you can say this, you have to know where you are going. A young man is not ready to be married if he lacks specific goals, if he has not settled on a general direction in life. Know where you are going before you ask a young lady to commit herself to following you.

Are you ready to lead spiritually? Are you able and willing to establish a home solidly built upon the principles of God's Word? Are you committed to taking your family faithfully to a good, Bible-preaching church? Are you strong in your knowledge of the Bible and in the convictions that you have established as a result of studying God's Word?

Do you understand the difference between being a leader and being a dictator? Are you willing to seek your wife's input before making each decision and then carefully consider how your final decisions will affect her? Do you love her with a love that would sacrifice self in order to protect her and provide for her needs?

"I am prepared to leave."

Marriage births a new family unit. *"Therefore shall a man leave his father and his mother, and shall cleave unto his wife: and they shall be one flesh"* (Genesis 2:24).

When young people talk about leaving home, they often use the word *freedom*, as in, "I can't wait until I'm able to move out and have my freedom!"

Don't miss what I am about to say. *The word freedom is spelled r-e-s-p-o-n-s-i-b-i-l-i-t-y.* Forming a new family unit is a *great responsibility.* Young man, if you feel you are ready to get married, then you are saying that you are ready to "cut the apron strings." You are mentally, physically, emotionally, financially and spiritually ready to step out on your own and start and support your own family. The children this marriage produces are your and your wife's responsibility to rear, not your parents' responsibility (and not that of some day-care providers!). The monthly bills are your responsibility to pay. Life's problems are your responsibility to solve. You will have freedom — the freedom to work long, hard days, the freedom to pay bills, the freedom of overcoming financial setbacks, the freedom to face and solve your marriage problems, the freedom to fix the car when it breaks down, the freedom to pay medical and dental bills, and the freedom to deal with the ever-changing stages of your children as they grow and develop.

Do you have to do this alone? No! Thankfully the Lord is there, and there is the emotional and physical support of extended family. But remember, you must bear the RESPONSIBILITY of loving, supporting and protecting this family unit. I am not trying to make this sound like drudgery. The privilege of being a husband and father is the greatest gift, outside of salvation, that God has ever given me — but it is not a game. You become the problem solver and financial provider of a new family unit. It is not up to your parents or anyone else to carry the responsibility that goes along with it. You cannot go running home to Mommy and Daddy every time something goes wrong.

"For every man shall bear his own burden" (Gal 6:5).

Welcome to freedom!

"I am prepared to provide."

It would surprise you to find out how many young men enter into marriage without a solid, workable financial plan. When you ask a young lady's father for her hand in marriage, you ought to be able to hand him a well- planned budget showing that you are financially capable of providing her with a decent home and the needs of life. Do you possess a viable, wage-earning skill? Are you currently making enough money to take on the responsibility of maintaining a household?

"For which of you, intending to build a tower, sitteth not down first, and counteth the cost" (Luke 14:28).

Sit down with your father and ask him to educate you on the amount of money it takes to establish your own home. List all of the weekly, monthly and quarterly bills that you must pay, and then add 25% to that so that you will be prepared for those unplanned expenses. After doing this, you must honestly ask yourself, "Am I in a position to establish a new household, or do I need more time to build up my resources or increase my earning power?" Most of the time, it is wise to finish your education and get established in your line of work before getting married.

The Prepared Young Woman

Likewise, young lady, before you say "I do," you should be able to honestly make these three statements:

"I am prepared to follow my husband."

"Wives, submit yourselves unto your own husbands, as unto the Lord" (Ephesians 5:22).

In many ways, it takes a greater depth of spirituality to follow than it does to lead. Before you rush to the marriage altar, you should carefully examine yourself in this area of submissiveness. A young lady who spends her teen years resisting and resenting the authority of her parents will spend her adult years fighting against the authority of her husband. Are you spiritually mature enough to follow?

"I am prepared to help my husband accomplish what God has called him to do."

"And the Lord God said, It is not good that the man should be alone; I will make him an help meet for him" (Genesis 2:18).

Eve was created to be a helpmeet for Adam. You are to be your husband's helper. A godly wife is concerned with making her husband a success, concerned with helping him to fulfill his calling in life. This is your career.

"I am prepared to manage a new household, to be the 'keeper' of our home."

"I will therefore that the younger women marry, bear children, guide the house, give none occasion to the adversary to speak reproachfully" (I Timothy 5:14).

"That they may teach the young women to be sober, to love their husbands, to love their children, To be discreet, chaste, keepers at home, good, obedient to their own husbands, that the word of God be not blasphemed" (Titus 2:4-5).

You must be trained in proper, efficient home management.

It takes an enormous amount of divine wisdom and practical skill to run a happy, efficient, cost-effective, God-centered home. Are you ready to be a "home-maker"?

5 Questions to Ask Before Getting Married Right Out of High School

Are you planning to get your high school diploma in May and your wedding license in June — of the same year? I want to challenge you to be prepared, to give your mate a spouse who is ready to take on the responsibilities of matrimony and parenthood. Here are some things to consider before trading in your high school cap and gown for a wedding tux or train.

Is that one you are considering conformed or transformed? Has he/she been living by Biblical standards and convictions because of the rules of his/her parents or the Christian school he/she attends, or simply conforming with no intention of later living a separated, dedicated life? Only *time* will tell!

Can you really live on love? Very few young men are financially ready to support a wife and establish an independent home one month after graduating from high school. Does real love ask a young lady to do without just because you want your carnal appetites satisfied?

Is this decision really about God's perfect will or your own sense of insecurity? "But if I wait, he/she might find someone else!" Faith does not speak in these terms but wholly follows God and trusts Him to work out His will in His time.

Will you regret missing your "thirteenth year"? I firmly believe that every Christian young person should attend Bible college for at least one year. This "thirteenth year" of education will give you a chance to meet other Christian young people, will deepen your commitment to Christ and will cushion the transition from living at home to living on your own by giving you a year of controlled independence in a safe, godly environment.

How different will you look at this decision in three years? Are you nearly 18 years of age? If so, think back to when you were 15. How much have you advanced in maturity since then? Now, multiply that by ten! *In your lifetime, there is no four-year time period in which your perception of yourself, of others, of God and of life will change any more than between 18 and 21 years of age.* Wouldn't it be wise to wait a few years before making the second most important decision of your life?

Marriage is a Lifelong Commitment

Here is a thought: if you are contemplating marriage, perhaps it would be good to schedule an afternoon to go off by yourself and spend a few hours reading and meditating upon the wedding vows. Study all of the words the preacher will say before you say "I do." Prayerfully consider each phrase you must repeat and agree to keep. Here is a copy of the standard set of the "repeat after me" part of the vows used in a Christian wedding.

A Husband's Vow to His Bride "I (groom's name) take thee (bride's name) to be my wedded wife, to have and to hold, from this day forward, for better for worse, for richer for poorer, in sickness and in health, to love and cherish, till death do us part."

A Bride's Vow to Her Husband "I (bride's name) take thee (groom's name) to be my wedded husband, to have and to hold, from this day forward, for better for worse, for richer for poorer, in sickness and in health, to love, cherish and obey, till death do us part."

These sacred offerings are called wedding "vows" because that is what they are! When two people make these wedding vows, they swear an oath that binds their souls to each other with an unbreakable bond. Read them again. These are not just empty words but solemn promises, holy commitments made to each other before Almighty God — and He expects you to keep them. So make sure you are ready!

"If a man vow a vow unto the Lord, or swear an oath to bind his soul with a bond; he shall not break his word, he shall do according to all that proceedeth out of his mouth" (Numbers 30:2).

4

Fourth Royal Law of Courtship

"By the grace of Almighty God, our marriage will have the blessing of both sets of parents and our pastors."

I do not agree with or condone arranged marriages. I think that the idea of two sets of parents espousing their son and daughter to each other is ludicrous. There are some extreme teachings floating around that attempt to equate ancient Jewish customs with inspired Scriptural instruction. This is not "sound doctrine" and, as a result, it does not produce sound results.

I do believe that a wise young person will lean heavily on his parents' counsel and insight during the courting process. If you are blessed to have dedicated Christian parents, you would be foolish not to access their wisdom and experience. Consider these Biblical principles as you think about the importance of securing the blessing of your parents and pastor.

Counsel is essential when you are dealing with matters of the heart.

"Hear counsel, and receive instruction, that thou mayest be wise in the latter end. There are many devices in a man's heart; nevertheless the counsel of the Lord, that shall stand" (Proverbs 19:20-21).

"He that trusteth in his own heart is a fool: but whoso walketh wisely, he shall be delivered" (Proverbs 28:26).

One of the most popular pieces of advice that the world propagates over and over through its movies and its music is this: ***follow your heart***. "If you don't know what to do, listen to your heart, and you'll never go wrong." Interesting. That counsel may sound good and certainly appeals to the pride of mankind, but it is just opposite of what the Bible teaches. God states that if you trust in your own heart, you are a fool.

It is important to understand that our hearts are capable of "many devices." Our emotions can often override our own good judgment. Be careful! Sometimes we feel so strongly that it makes it hard to think straight. That is why God has provided us with a "safety net" called counsel.

"Where no counsel is, the people fall: but in the multitude of counsellors there is safety" (Proverbs 11:14).

"Without counsel purposes are disappointed: but in the multitude of counsellors they are established" (Proverbs 15:22).

Counsel will keep you from falling, and it will prevent disappointments. There is safety in a multitude of counselors. Don't try to work through this complicated, emotional maze called life without the help of the wise people God has put over you and around you.

No two people in the world know you better than your parents.

Because this is true, the "chief counselors" in your cabinet of wise counselors should be your parents.

Give your parents veto power.

If your parents strongly feel that a certain young person you are attracted to is not God's will for your life, listen to them.

"And he [Samson] *came up, and told his father and his mother, and said, I have seen a woman in Timnath of the daughters of the Philistines: now therefore get her for me to wife. Then his father and his mother said unto him, Is there never a woman among the daughters of thy brethren, or among all my people, that thou goest to take a wife of the uncircumcised Philistines? And Samson said unto his father, Get her for me; for she pleaseth me well"* (Judges 14:2-3)

Had Samson listened to the suggestions of his parents, he would not have spent a good part of his life blindly grinding corn for the Philistines. Many a young person has lived to regret not listening to the advice of his parents when seeking a marriage partner.

"The way of a fool is right in his own eyes: but he that hearkeneth unto counsel is wise" (Proverbs 12:15).

Beware of anyone who tries to drive a wedge between you and your parents.

"My son, keep thy father's commandment, and forsake not the law of thy mother: Bind them continually upon thine heart, and tie them about thy neck. When thou goest, it shall lead thee; when thou sleepest, it shall keep thee; and when thou awakest, it shall talk with thee.... To keep thee from the evil woman, from the flattery of the tongue of a strange woman" (Proverbs 6:20-24).

I have always found suspect a young person who is possessive and controlling in his treatment of another young person. God loves us and asks that we love Him but He also encourages us to love our families and friends. He does not demand that our love be exclusively directed to Him — and He is God! If a young person tries to turn your affection away from your parents by criticizing their rules and beliefs, get away from him/her. The right relationship with the person who is God's perfect will for your life will strengthen your other relationships, not destroy them. Weak and insecure is the person who constantly strives to control others. This person will not make a good marriage partner.

Wise parents will encourage their child to seek the counsel of their pastor during the courting process.

Parents, remember that we too are heavily invested emotionally in our children. We should be! But that also can sometimes cloud our judgment. I believe that is why the Scripture instructs us — for safety — to have a multitude of counselors. A good pastor "knows the state of his flock." Utilize his wise counsel and input as this important decision is made in the life of your child.

If your child meets someone at Bible college, be sure to contact the pastor of the young person your child is interested in. Sometimes a pastor knows some important information about that young person (a record of promiscuity, an abortion, homosexual tendencies, rebellion, habitual lying, laziness, indebtedness, etc.) that would cause you to consider carefully not encouraging your son/daughter to pursue a close relationship. Sometimes, because of confidentiality reasons, that pastor may not be able to give you specifics, so you must learn to trust him if he cautions against the pairing but does not share with you all his reasons.

I knew a pastor who did this very thing when asked about a

possible marriage partner for a young lady. He cautioned the parents and the young lady against pursuing this relationship, but would not give them specifics. He couldn't because what he had learned was learned in strict confidence. The family chose to ignore his warnings, and a few years after their daughter had married the young man, he ran off with someone else. That someone else was another guy! The pastor had been privy to these tendencies, and had the family heeded his warning, they could have spared themselves a world of heartache.

Secure the blessing of both sets of parents. Secure the blessing of both pastors. This provides safety and protection for both young people involved.

"Every purpose is established by counsel" (Proverbs 20:18).

5
Fifth Royal Law of Courtship

"By the grace of Almighty God, I will have glorified God and maintained an unquestionable Christian testimony throughout my courtship."

The primary purpose of our existence as Christians is to bring glory to God. A wise young person is constantly aware of his/her Christian testimony. Both the saved and the lost watch any young person who professes to know the Lord as his/her Saviour, but never are you more under the microscope than when you are courting. Whether or not that is fair, I don't know — but I am telling you that it is true. Your conduct during courtship will either show all who are watching how real and precious Jesus is to you, or it will bring a shadow of reproach upon His precious name.

1. Avoid the appearances of evil.

"Abstain from all appearance of evil" (I The 5:22).

Mature Christian thinking does not just ask, "Is what we are doing wrong?" It also asks, "Could what we are doing appear wrong to others?"

There is a brand of root beer I don't drink. They sell it in bottles that look like brown beer bottles. It would not be a sin to drink it — it is root beer! However, drinking it could damage my testimony because from a distance, it gives the appearance of evil.

While you are courting, be as concerned with the appearance of right as you are with the doing of right.

"Let not then your good be evil spoken of" (Rom 14:16).

2. Protect carefully the reputation of the one you are courting.

"Charity vaunteth not itself, is not puffed up, Doth not behave itself unseemly, seeketh not her own" (I Corinthians 13:4-5).

One of the evidences of true love is the intense desire to protect the one you care about. If someone truly loves you, he would never ask anything of you that might have the potential of casting a shadow across your reputation. Lust seeks its own and thinks nothing of unseemly behavior. Love makes its decisions based on what is best for the other individual and is always aware of protecting his/her reputation.

3. Exalt Christ in your relationship.

"And he is the head of the body, the church: who is the beginning, the firstborn from the dead; that in all things he might have the preeminence" (Colossians 1:18).

Honor Christ in all that you do. Proudly wear the name "Christian" and let it spill over into every area of your life. Why not have a relationship that glorifies and honors the name of Christ? Do you not think that He will, in return, honor such a relationship?

4. Build all your relationships on a rock — the solid foundation of clear Biblical teaching.

"Therefore whosoever heareth these sayings of mine, and doeth them, I will liken him unto a wise man, which built his house upon a rock" (Matthew 7:24-27).

One of the advantages of building anything on the foundation of Bible principles is that you know it will stand the test of time. If in foolish pride you choose to ignore what the Bible teaches and do it "your way" (which is not your way, but the world's way), then you are building upon the sand. Divorces are a dime a dozen. When the house falls, you will wish you had considered all of the verses that you have read in this short book.

6
Sixth Royal Law of Courtship

"By the grace of Almighty God, I will to give my partner someone who understands and practices real agape love."

The Bible Definition of Love

There is only one place in the Bible where I find a definition of love. Many places in the Bible describe love or illustrate love, but there is only one place I have found where it is specifically defined.

"God is love" (I John 4:8).

I know. To a teenager, that probably doesn't sound very romantic. You were hoping for something like "Love is the cascading of pure human emotions falling down as a waterfall into the very pool of your soul" or something you would find on a poster at the mall or in a Hallmark card. But the truth is, you will never find a more romantic definition of love than "*God is love.*"

To have a relationship with another person and to be able to love them with a love that is divine — God-sent and God-empowered — is the greatest gift that can be shared between two people. God is the original romantic. The only reason any of us can love is because we were created in his image. We can love because He first loved us. To pursue a relationship that excludes God is to pursue a relationship that is loveless.

Learning to Recognize Biblical Love

I am going to give you a big assignment. If you look in an exhaustive Bible concordance, you can find a listing of every place in the Bible where the word "love" (or some form of it) is found. There are over 550 places where it is found. If you want to understand how biblical love thinks, responds, acts and conducts itself, look these verses up and read them in their context. Then keep a notebook and write down what each of these verses teaches you about love. You do not have to do them all at once. Try five verses a day before you go to bed each night. If you do this, you can have this project completed in less than four months. And at the end of that four months, I believe you will have the ability to recognize true Bible love a mile away. Even more importantly, you will be able to recognize a cheap counterfeit!

"Study to shew thyself approved unto God, a workman that needeth not to be ashamed, rightly dividing the word of truth" (II Timothy 2:15).

Do a Careful Study of the Love Chapter

I Corinthians, chapter 13, has long been called "the love chapter." You might be shocked to find that the word love is not found in this chapter. Instead, the Greek word *agape* has been translated *charity*. *Agape* is a Greek word meaning "divine love" or "God-love." It is the strongest, truest and deepest of all forms of human affection.

Let's look at what this chapter teaches about love.

Verse 1: *"Though I speak with the tongues of men and of angels, and have not charity, I am become as sounding brass, or a tinkling cymbal."*

Love is more than words. Spoken words, no matter how beautifully delivered, can be said without true love behind them. When that is the case, the best framed sentences and most carefully delivered orations take on the irritating sounds of clanging brass and clanking cymbals.

Verse 2: *And though I have the gift of prophecy, and understand all mysteries, and all knowledge; and though I have all faith, so that I could remove mountains, and have not charity, I am nothing."*

Love is more than being spiritual. The sad truth is, there are many Christians who have spent much time in developing the depths of their Bible knowledge and have even exercised that knowledge by stepping out by faith and accomplishing amazing things, but they have neglected to develop the most essential fruit of the Spirit in their life — love. And because of that, they are nothing.

Verse 3: *"And though I bestow all my goods to feed the poor, and though I give my body to be burned, and have not charity, it profiteth me nothing."*

Love is more than sacrifice. It is possible to perform acts of benevolence even to the point of sacrificing one's own life for another, yet not do it from a heart filled with divine love. When it happens this way, it profits nothing for eternity.

These first three verses are not condemning spoken words, spiritual knowledge, acts of faith or personal sacrifice. They are saying that all these things can be performed outside the catalyst of divine love — and when they are, they are empty and meaningless. So be careful. Often the presence of these is mistaken as evidence of true love.

"He loves me!" How do you know?

"He says the sweetest things, and he is so spiritual and always doing the nicest things for me and others. He even told me he would give his life for me."

OK. But remember, these are not evidences of love. Love may be the motive behind them, but all of these things can be done without real agape love as the driving force behind them.

"Then what are the true evidences of real love?"

Glad you asked. Let's keep reading.

Verse 4: *"Charity suffereth long, and is kind; charity envieth not; charity vaunteth not itself, is not puffed up."*

Love is patient. Love is kind. Love does not envy. Love does not promote self. Love is not prideful.

Verse 5: *"Doth not behave itself unseemly, seeketh not her own, is not easily provoked, thinketh no evil."*

Love does not behave indecently or shamefully. Love is not selfish or self-centered. Love does not have a short fuse. Love does not premeditate to do wrong.

Verse 6: *"Rejoiceth not in iniquity, but rejoiceth in the truth."*

Love gets excited about the right things. It does not rejoice in sinfulness, but instead in the truths of God's Word.

Verse 7: *"Beareth all things, believeth all things, hopeth all things, endureth all things."*

Love is strong; it does not quit when things get hard. **Love is trusting;** it looks for the good instead of the bad. **Love is optimistic**; it trusts God for tomorrow. **Love is tough;** it endures instead of complains.

Verse 8. *"Charity never faileth."*

Love commits! Because of that, it does not fail.

A person can have a velvet tongue, may seem to be filled with great Bible knowledge and faith, and be constantly sacrificing and giving to others, but...

If they are not patient and kind, they lack love.

If they are envious of others, they lack love.

If they are full of pride and constantly talking about self, they lack love.

If they behave indecently or in a way that brings shame to the Lord, they lack love.

If they are selfish and self-centered, they lack love.

If they are quick-tempered, they lack love.

If they are always trying to figure out how to get by with wrong, they lack love.

If they enjoy wrong and disdain right, they lack love.

If they are quick to quit, distrusting, pessimistic and constantly complaining, they lack love.

So many of the deficiencies in our character could be overcome if we would just take the time to discover the true meaning of biblical love and practice it every moment of every day towards all people. Then, and only then, would we have a taste of what it is like to be divine.

Watch Out for Counterfeits!

I want to speak a moment directly to the heart of the young ladies reading this book. Countless times in my twenty-plus years of working with teenagers, I have watched young ladies be fooled by counterfeit love. I am now thinking of several young ladies who, in my mind, were destined to be used in a great way for the Lord Jesus Christ; but Satan sent into their lives someone who showed them a little attention, beguiled them with romantic words and gestures, and then stole their purity. After these predators were finished with them, they left these sweet young ladies brokenhearted at best and pregnant at worst. Then they went on their way to find another gullible teenage girl to deceive.

Young lady, God has something better planned for your life! If you have not read my booklet *Stay in the Castle*, order it and read it.

I have found that the young ladies who are most easily susceptible to falling for a counterfeit are those of you who are reared in homes where biblical love is not available to you or modeled before you. What a tragedy for a child to be reared in a home where she is not loved! If this is true of you, you have to be especially vigilant. All of us hunger for attention. Everyone wants to feel special to someone. Be careful! Satan knows this and will send the wrong type of person into your life! This counterfeit will show you some special attention, say all the right things and, if you are not careful, convince you that he loves you when the truth is that all he wants to do is use you.

If you are right now in a relationship that is not healthy — is not based on biblical love and is not in the perfect time frame of God's will — have the courage to break it off! Then be patient, follow Bible principles and seek godly counsel before ever going forward into another such relationship.

I could fill up this book with horror stories, the terrible results of young ladies who were blinded by the desire to be loved yet who failed to recognize until it was too late that what they were willing to settle for was not true love.

Seek the Fullness of the Holy Spirit.

"But the fruit of the Spirit is love" (Galatians 5:22).

"Be filled with the Spirit" (Ephesians 5:18).

God is love. We have established that. The Holy Spirit is the person of the triune God that indwells us as believers. He produces love in us and through us. The more we surrender ourselves to his leading, the more the fruit of love will be evident in our daily lives.

We are commanded to be filled with the Spirit. This does not mean that we get more of Him; it means He gets all of us. Young person, before you will ever be able to practice true agape love, you must empty yourself of sin and self and surrender fully to the control of the Holy Spirit. Let Him lead you, and you will never go wrong.

Your future mate deserves someone who has taken the time to understand and practice true *agape* love. Take that time. In doing so, you will be transformed! And you will be ready to give your future partner a love that "never faileth."

7
Tenants of the Seventh Royal Law of Courtship

"By the grace of Almighty God, on my wedding day, I will be in a position to fulfill God's specific calling for my life."

I want to say a word to those of you who are called into some type of full-time Christian service. Perhaps a young man is reading this whom God has called to the mission field or to be a pastor or an evangelist. If the call of God is upon your life to preach the Gospel full-time, you have been given a serious and blessed charge. As Paul said, *"Yea, woe is unto me, if I preach not the gospel"* (I Corinthians 9:16).

First, let me say, you need a good wife. *"It is not good that the man should be alone"*. You need a helpmeet to work with you and beside you in the ministry. *"Whoso findeth a wife findeth a good thing, and obtaineth favour of the Lord"* (Proverbs 18:22). God even lists as one of the requirements of a bishop that he be *"the husband of one wife"* (Titus 1:6).

But you need to be very careful as you seek God's will in selecting that helpmeet. Satan would like nothing better than to let your decision concerning *whom* you marry or *when* you marry postpone or eliminate your ability to fulfill your calling. Carefully consider this advice, and may God bless you as you pursue your calling.

1. It is best to finish your schooling (Bible college) before you get married.

2. Make sure that the young lady you are considering has dedicated her life to the Lord's work.

3. Do not marry someone who is materialistically minded. You cannot serve God and mammon.

4. Do not marry someone who is selfish by nature. Full-time work requires a willingness to give of oneself. There is no room for selfishness in the Lord's work.

5. Stay focused on your calling. If you have to leave the pursuit of your calling in order to pursue a young lady, she is the wrong one. God will bring you your Eve in His time, along the

path of obedience to your calling.

****

In this booklet I have shared with you principles founded on the Word of God. They are right and true. It takes courage and commitment to turn your back on the worldly mainstream dating philosophies that have cost so many good teenagers their innocence and long-term happiness. For the sake of that one who is out there praying for the day when you will meet, I challenge you to embrace what many would consider old-fashioned and outdated ideas, and to bear the scorn and misunderstanding of those who will always settle for less.

Are you must be willing to enact the seven royal laws of courtship? If you decide to live by these laws, they will guide you past the snares of Satan and the pitfalls of your own humanity, and someday into the arms of that one whom God has created for you. Don't miss that divine appointment.

Satan is great about snatching the seed that has been planted in our hearts before it has a chance to take root. I firmly believe the old proverb "Out of sight, out of mind." Your decision to incorporate these seven biblical principles into your life will soon be forgotten if you do not regularly recommit yourself to the truths they contain. On the following page, I have provided for you a pledge that you may want to fill out and then cut from the pages of this booklet and affix somewhere in your room where you will see it at the beginning of each day.

God speed to you as you continue on your journey toward God's perfect will for your life and, eventually, God's perfect choice for your life.

My Pledge to Almighty God and to That Someone, Somewhere, Who Awaits Me

1. By the grace of Almighty God, I will marry the person God has created for me.
2. By the grace of Almighty God, I will arrive at the marriage altar morally pure.
3. By the grace of Almighty God, I will arrive at the marriage altar prepared to fulfill my responsibilities as a marriage partner.
4. By the grace of Almighty God, our marriage will have the blessing of both sets of parents and our pastors.
5. By the grace of Almighty God, I will have glorified God and maintained an unquestionable Christian testimony throughout my courtship.
6. By the grace of Almighty God, I will give to my partner someone who understands and practices real agape love.
7. By the grace of Almighty God, on my wedding day, I will be in a position to fulfill God's specific calling for my life.

Each day I will pray for you, each day I will wait for you, each day I will prepare for you. And one day, I will give you a part of my heart that I have reserved and protected for only you.

Signed this __seventh__ *day of the month of* __June__ *in the year of our Lord* __2022__ .

(signature)

Other Books by the Author

Seven Royal Laws of Courtship
The Teenage Years of Jesus Christ
The Childhood Years of Jesus Christ
The 21 Tenets of Biblical Femininity
The 21 Tenets of Biblical Masculinity
Is Your Youth Group Dead or Alive?
Mountain Lessons
Grace Will Lead Me Home
104 Teen Bible Lessons
Did God Put a Book Inside of You?

Stay in the Castle Series
Stay in the Castle
The Warrior Prince
The Chosen One
The Prodigals

The Teenager's Guide Series
A Teenager's Guide to Character, Success, & Happiness
A Teenager's Guide to the Invisible Creation
A Teenager's Guide to Healthy Relationships

Ultimate Goal Publications
Order by phone or online
(812) 665-4375
www.stayinthecastle.com